# E-Commerce Mastery: Building a Successful Online Store in 2023

# Table of content

**Chapter 1: Introduction to E-commerce: An Overview**

E-commerce, or electronic commerce, is the buying and selling of goods and services over the internet. With the digital revolution, e-commerce has become an integral part of the global retail framework. This chapter will provide an overview of the e-commerce landscape, including the different types of e-commerce models and the benefits and challenges of owning an online store.

**Chapter 2: Selecting Your Niche: Finding the Perfect Product**

Choosing the right product or service to sell is a crucial decision that can make or break your e-commerce business. This chapter will guide you on how to find profitable niches, perform market research, analyze competition, and validate your product idea.

**Chapter 3: E-commerce Platforms: Choosing Your Online Home**

An e-commerce platform is the backbone of any online retail business. This chapter will review the top e-commerce platforms in 2023, with a focus on their features, pricing, scalability, and ease of use.

**Chapter 4: Website Design: Building Your Online Storefront**

Having a well-designed, user-friendly website can significantly affect your sales and customer retention. This chapter will cover the fundamental principles of good e-commerce website design, including mobile optimization, usability, aesthetics, and site speed.

**Chapter 5: Search Engine Optimization: Drawing Traffic to Your Store**

SEO is vital in attracting organic traffic to your online store. This chapter will teach you how to optimize your website for search engines, create SEO-friendly content, build quality backlinks, and understand Google's algorithm updates.

## Chapter 6: Social Media Marketing: Building Your Brand

Social media is an essential tool for any e-commerce business. This chapter will explore the best practices for using different social media platforms, creating engaging content, running social media campaigns, and leveraging influencers to grow your brand.

## Chapter 7: Email Marketing: Engaging Your Customers

Email marketing is one of the most effective ways to engage customers and drive sales. This chapter will show you how to build your email list, segment your audience, craft compelling emails, and automate your email marketing campaigns.

## Chapter 8: Customer Service: Creating Lasting Relationships

Providing excellent customer service can set your business apart from competitors. This chapter will outline strategies for improving customer service, including managing customer complaints, providing effective communication, and implementing a customer-first approach.

## Chapter 9: Analytics: Tracking Your Success

Data and analytics can provide crucial insights into your business. This chapter will teach you how to set up analytics tracking, interpret data, make data-driven decisions, and understand key e-commerce metrics.

## Chapter 10: Logistics: Shipping and Handling

Handling the logistics of your e-commerce business can be challenging but necessary. This chapter will explore best practices for managing inventory, packing, shipping, handling returns, and choosing third-party logistics providers.

**Chapter 11: International Markets: Going Global**

If you're ready to take your business global, this chapter will help you navigate international e-commerce. Topics include understanding cross-border e-commerce

# Chapter 1

## Introduction to E-commerce: An Overview

Technology and digital transformation have brought rapid changes to business over the years, including significant advancements in electronic commerce (commonly referred to as e-commerce). E-commerce involves buying and selling goods over the internet and has quickly become part of the global retail framework.

This chapter provides an introduction to the e-commerce landscape, outlining different e-commerce models, benefits and challenges of owning an online store, key trends influencing this sector and industry outlook.

**Types of E-commerce Models**

There are four main types of e-commerce models:

- Business to Consumer (B2C): B2C e-commerce models arBusiness to Consumer (B2C): B2C is the most prevalent e-commerce model, where companies sell directly to individual consumers online - this model includes established retailers like Amazon and Walmart as examples of such businesses selling to individuals directly.

- Business to Business (B2B): Under this model, businesses sell directly to other businesses; typically this involves wholesale deals, enterprise software sales or bulk product purchases.

- Consumer to Consumer (C2C) transactions: Here, consumers sell directly to other consumers through platforms such as eBay or Etsy that facilitate peer-to-peer sales transactions.
- Consumer-to-Business (C2B): C2B refers to an emerging model where individuals offer products or services online directly for businesses to buy; examples may include crowdsourcing services, freelance services or affiliate marketing.

## Benefits of E-commerce

The e-commerce business model offers several benefits, including:

- Global reach: E-commerce allows businesses to reach customers from any part of the world without the physical constraints of a brick-and-mortar store.
- 24/7 Availability: Online stores are open around the clock, providing convenience for customers and increasing potential for sales.
- Lower Costs: E-commerce can be more cost-effective than traditional retail, as it often requires fewer overheads like rent, utilities, and staff.
- Data Collection: Online businesses have unique access to customer data, allowing for advanced analytics and better business decisions.

## Challenges of E-commerce

While e-commerce offers great potential, it also comes with its own set of challenges:

- Competition: The ease of starting an e-commerce business means that competition is fierce. Standing out requires innovation, exceptional service, and effective marketing.

- Customer Trust: Building trust with online customers can be challenging. You need to ensure safe payment methods, reliable service, and effective handling of data privacy.
- Shipping and Logistics: Managing inventory and shipping can be complex, especially for businesses that ship internationally.

## Key Trends in E-commerce

As 2023 approaches, the e-commerce landscape continues to shift and change. According to 2023 projections, key trends include increasing use of AI/ML for personalized shopping experiences, mobile commerce growth and the emergence of voice commerce platforms. Sustainable shopping as well as social commerce - transactions made directly via social media platforms - is also shaping this industry.

E-commerce is an engaging and dynamic field with unlimited potential. When embarking on this adventure, understanding its landscape is your first step; in the following chapter we'll look into selecting your niche and finding products suitable for an online store.

# Chapter 2

## Selecting Your Niche: Finding the Perfect Product

Step two of creating a successful e-commerce store involves finding your niche and product or service. This chapter will show you how to find profitable niches, conduct market research, evaluate competition and validate product ideas.

**Finding Your Niche**

Niche markets represent a specific category within a larger market for specific kinds of goods or services, so selecting an ideal niche is crucial to your online store's success. When making this selection, keep the following in mind:

1. Passion: Choose a niche you are passionate or interested about to stay motivated while working on products you enjoy using.
2. Profitability: To ensure profitability of your niche business venture, ensure there is enough demand to generate sales without becoming saturated and create too much competition for sales.
3. Knowledge: Gaining an in-depth knowledge of your niche will enable you to provide helpful content and solutions to customers. If this is something new for you, be prepared to learn quickly.

**Market Research**

Once you've identified a potential niche, the next step should be market research. This involves gathering data on your customers and competitors within it using online tools like Google Trends, SEMrush or Ahrefs.

**Analyzing the Competition**

Understanding your competitors is vital to the success of any e-commerce venture. Research their websites, prices, marketing strategies, customer reviews and unique selling proposition (USP). Doing this will allow you to differentiate your business and find its USP (unique selling proposition).

**Product Validation**

After conducting market research and assessing your competition, the next step should be validating your product idea. This process ensures there is genuine demand for it before investing more resources in it.

Product validation can be completed through various techniques such as keyword research, social media surveys or even pre-selling your product. The aim is to collect evidence showing that potential customers are interested and willing to pay for your offering.

Locating and selecting an appealing product or service to sell can make or break an e-commerce business. By conducting thorough research and carefully choosing products tailored specifically towards target audiences, success will become much easier to attain.

Next chapter we'll cover how to choose an e-commerce platform suitable for your online store - an essential step toward building a prosperous e-commerce business.

# Chapter 3

## E-commerce Platforms: Choosing Your Online Home

Your e-commerce platform is the cornerstone of your online retail business, serving as the hub for listing products, managing sales and engaging customers. Therefore, selecting one that best meets your business requirements, budget constraints and technical skills is of the utmost importance. In this chapter we review some of the leading e-commerce platforms of 2023 with regards to features such as pricing structure, scalability and ease of use.

**Selecting Your E-commerce Platform**

Several factors should guide your selection of an e-commerce platform:

1. Ease of use: A good platform should be easy to navigate, even for those without technical skills.
2. Pricing: Consider both the upfront and ongoing costs of using the platform.
3. Scalability: Ensure your chosen platform can grow with your business.
4. Customization: Look for a platform that allows for customization so your site can reflect your brand.

Integration: The platform should integrate well with other systems you use, like email marketing software or inventory management tools.

**Top E-commerce Platforms in 2023**

1. Shopify: As one of the premier ecommerce platforms, Shopify stands out with its user-friendly interface, customizable templates and robust set of features. Offering everything needed to establish and run an online store successfully, this platform makes Shopify an excellent option for both newcomers and experienced retailers.

2. WooCommerce: WooCommerce is a free, open-source e-commerce plugin for WordPress that has quickly become one of the go-to choices among businesses looking to combine content marketing and e-commerce, or already possessing one.

3. BigCommerce: BigCommerce provides businesses of all sizes a comprehensive platform designed to support multichannel selling across social media channels and marketplaces. The built-in features enable multichannel selling across various social platforms.

4. Magento: Magento is an effective e-commerce platform best suited for mid to large sized businesses, as its open-source nature provides immense customizability while still requiring some technical know-how for optimal use.

5. Wix eCommerce: Wix eCommerce is an ideal choice for small businesses or startups, being user-friendly with customizable templates and an easy drag-and-drop interface for customization.

**Final Thoughts**

Selecting an e-commerce platform is a major decision that can have lasting ramifications on the efficiency, customer experience, and overall success of your business. Take the time to research each of the available platforms carefully before selecting one that aligns with your goals and capabilities.

Next chapter we will dive deeper into the fundamental principles of good e-commerce website design to ensure a visually appealing yet user-friendly store online.

# Chapter 4

## Website Design: Building Your Online Storefront

Your e-commerce website is your online storefront, and its design can significantly affect your sales and customer retention. A well-designed website is not only aesthetically pleasing but also user-friendly, mobile-optimized, and fast-loading. In this chapter, we'll cover the fundamental principles of good e-commerce website design.

**User Experience (UX)**

At the heart of successful e-commerce website design is a strong focus on user experience. Your site should be intuitive and easy to navigate. Here are some key principles of UX design:

- Simplicity: Keep your design simple, clean, and uncluttered. The quicker a customer can find what they're looking for, the better.
- Consistency: Ensure consistency across your site in terms of fonts, colors, and style to provide a smooth experience for your visitors.
- Navigation: Your site's navigation should be clear and easily accessible, with a search function to help customers find products quickly.

**Mobile Optimization**

With a large number of consumers shopping on their mobile devices, mobile optimization is crucial. A mobile-friendly site adapts and displays correctly on smaller screens and offers easy navigation for touchscreens.

**Aesthetics**

Your website's design can greatly influence visitors' perceptions of your brand. Your design should reflect this, appealing to both target audiences and your own image of what constitutes successful branding. Employing high-quality images, professional product photos, and videos for an engaging website experience.

**Website Speed**

Slow-loading websites can frustrate customers and lead to high bounce rates. Optimize your site's speed by compressing images, using a reliable hosting provider, and regularly monitoring your site's speed.

**Product Pages**

Your product pages should provide comprehensive and compelling information about their offerings, such as high-quality photos from multiple angles, detailed product descriptions, customer reviews and clear pricing and shipping information.

**Secure Checkout Process**

To build customer trust and reduce cart abandonment, ensure your checkout process is secure, fast, and seamless. Offer various payment options and consider implementing a guest checkout option for customers who don't wish to create an account.

**Call-to-Action (CTA) Buttons**

CTA buttons guide users towards taking a desired action, like "Add to Cart" or "Buy Now." Make your CTAs prominent, clear, and compelling to boost conversions.

Designing an effective e-commerce website can be a complex task, but it's an essential component of your online success. Keep your customers at the forefront of your design decisions, and aim to create a seamless, enjoyable online shopping experience.

In the next chapter, we'll explore how to draw traffic to your store through search engine optimization.

# Chapter 5

## Search Engine Optimization: Drawing Traffic to Your Store

Search Engine Optimization (SEO) is an essential element of e-commerce business success. SEO refers to making your website more visible in search engine results, increasing traffic significantly to your online store. In this chapter, we will cover how to optimize your site for search engines by creating SEO-friendly content, building quality backlinks and understanding Google's algorithm updates.

**On-Page SEO**

On-page SEO refers to the practice of optimizing individual web pages on your site. This includes:

1. Keywords: Keywords are the words or phrases that users type into search engines. Your goal is to identify relevant keywords that potential customers might use to find your products, and then incorporate these keywords naturally into your site's content and meta tags.
2. Meta Tags: Meta tags are snippets of text that describe a page's content. They don't appear on the page itself, but in the page's HTML code. Meta tags can impact a page's ranking and how it appears in search results.
3. URL Structure: URLs should be easy to read and include relevant keywords where possible.

Internal Linking: Linking to other pages on your site helps search engines understand the content of your site and can improve your site's visibility in search results.

## Content Creation

Quality content plays a significant role in SEO. Regularly updating your site with fresh, relevant content can help improve your search rankings. Blog posts, buying guides, and videos can all attract visitors and keep them on your site longer, improving your site's "dwell time," a factor that can impact SEO.

## Backlinks

Backlinks are links from other websites to your site. They're a crucial part of SEO because they signal to search engines that other sites vouch for your content. Earning quality backlinks can improve your site's credibility and boost your visibility in search results.

## Understanding Algorithm Updates

Search engines continually update their algorithms to provide users with the most relevant results. Staying current with these updates can help you adjust your SEO strategy as needed. Google's algorithm updates are especially important to pay attention to, as Google dominates the search engine market.

**Local SEO**

If your store or target demographic are geographically focused, local SEO should also be taken into consideration. This may involve tactics such as targeting relevant local keywords for optimization purposes and claiming your listing on Google My Business while managing online reviews.

Effective SEO strategies can substantially boost traffic to your online store, leading to more leads and sales. Although SEO requires ongoing commitment, its payoff can be significant. In the next chapter, we'll look at building brand identity through social media marketing.

# Chapter 6

## Social Media Marketing: Building Your Brand and Community

Social media has quickly become an essential business tool in today's digital landscape, providing an invaluable platform to promote products, engage customers, and increase brand recognition. This chapter will walk you through creating a social media strategy, selecting suitable platforms for your business needs, creating engaging content for each platform used, and tracking success metrics.

**Creating a Social Media Strategy**

An effective social media strategy provides guidance for your actions and allows you to gauge if they're succeeding or failing. Here are the key steps in developing such a plan:

1. Set Goals: What do you hope to accomplish through social media efforts? This could include increasing brand recognition, driving website visitors or increasing product sales.
2. Establish Your Target Audience: Who are your potential customers? Understanding their demographics, interests and online behavior will enable you to create content they'll interact with.
3. Select Your Social Media Platforms: Not all social media platforms will be appropriate for your business; select those where your target audience frequents most often.

4. Plan Your Content: Create a content calendar so you can plan what and when you will share content - this will make posting easier while making efforts more manageable.

**Choosing the Right Platforms**

There are numerous social media platforms available, each with its unique user demographics and strengths:

1. Facebook: With such a broad user base, Facebook provides businesses a versatile platform that is ideal for both organic posts and paid advertising.
2. Instagram: As the visual platform it is perfect for businesses that rely heavily on images such as fashion, art, food and travel businesses.
3. Twitter: Twitter provides businesses with an excellent way of sharing news, engaging with customers, and managing customer service. Pinterest: Pinterest can serve as an excellent source of visual inspiration; making it ideal for creative businesses such as interior design, fashion or cooking industries.
4. LinkedIn: For B2B businesses, LinkedIn can be an invaluable platform for networking and sharing industry news and insights.

**Creating Engaging Content**

Creation of content that resonates with your target audience is paramount for social media success. This could include product photos, how-to videos, customer testimonials, behind-the-scenes looks at your business or educational posts related to your industry.

**Tracking Your Success**

Utilize social media analytics tools to evaluate the success of your efforts on social media. Measure metrics such as engagement rate, click-through rate, conversion rate or follower growth - use this data to refine and enhance your strategy over time and achieve better results!

Social media can be an extremely effective tool in building your e-commerce business. When employed correctly and strategically, it can reach more customers, strengthen brand recognition, and generate additional sales.

In the next chapter, we'll investigate how email marketing can increase conversions and encourage repeat business.

# Chapter 7

## Email Marketing: Nurturing Leads and Driving Repeat Business

Email marketing is an indispensable asset to your ecommerce arsenal, enabling you to engage directly with customers, nurture leads, drive sales and build long-term relationships. In this chapter, we will walk through how to build an email list, compose engaging emails and understand key email marketing metrics.

### Building Your Email List

Before you can start sending out emails, you need to build your email list. Here are a few effective ways to do this:

1. Lead Magnets: Offer something valuable in exchange for a visitor's email address, like a discount, free shipping, or a valuable piece of content.
2. Email Sign-Up Forms: Place email sign-up forms strategically on your website, like on your homepage, product pages, or at checkout.
3. Social Media Promotions: Promote your lead magnet or sign-up form on your social media channels.

### Crafting Engaging Emails

The success of your email marketing efforts depends on the quality of your emails. Here's how to craft emails that engage and convert:

- Subject Line: Your subject line is the first thing recipients see, so make it compelling and enticing to increase open rates.
- Personalization: Personalized emails can lead to higher engagement rates. Use your subscriber's name, recommend products based on past purchases, or send birthday discounts.
- Clear CTA: Each email should have a clear call-to-action (CTA), guiding readers on what to do next.
- Mobile Optimization: Many people check their email on their phones, so ensure your emails look good on smaller screens.

## Types of Emails

There are several types of emails you might send, each serving a different purpose:

- Welcome Emails: Send these after someone signs up for your email list, welcoming them and often providing a special offer.
- Promotional Emails: These emails highlight specific products, discounts, or special events.
- Abandoned Cart Emails: If a customer leaves items in their cart without checking out, send an email reminding them and maybe offering a discount to encourage completion of the purchase.
- Re-Engagement Emails: If a subscriber hasn't interacted with your emails in a while, send a re-engagement email to spark their interest.

## Email Marketing Metrics

Key metrics to track include open rate, click-through rate, conversion rate, and unsubscribe rate. These will give you insight into the effectiveness of your emails and where there might be room for improvement.

Email marketing, when done correctly, is a highly effective way to drive repeat business and build a loyal customer base. In the next chapter, we'll explore how to provide exceptional customer service to increase customer satisfaction and loyalty.

# Chapter 8

## Customer Service: Ensuring Satisfaction and Building Loyalty

Superior customer service is integral to any successful e-commerce store, not only solving customer issues but also cultivating loyalty among your customer base and strengthening brand image. In this chapter, you will learn how to establish a customer-centric culture, implement effective customer service practices, and manage customer feedback effectively.

**Creating a Customer-Centric Culture**

Every interaction a customer has with your business contributes to their overall perception of your brand. Therefore, it's essential to create a culture that prioritizes customer satisfaction. This involves:

1. Understanding Your Customers: Know who your customers are, what they want, and what their pain points might be.
2. Training Your Team: Make sure every team member understands the importance of customer service and how to interact with customers effectively.
3. Setting Service Standards: Set clear expectations for customer service and hold your team accountable.

**Effective Customer Service Practices**

Here are some practices to ensure your customers receive top-tier service:

1. Accessible Support: Make it easy for customers to reach you through multiple channels, such as email, phone, live chat, and social media.
2. Quick Response Times: Prompt responses show your customers that you value their time and are eager to assist.
3. Problem Resolution: Strive to resolve issues quickly and effectively. If a mistake is made, own up to it and find ways to make it right.
4. Personalization: Personalized service can significantly enhance customer satisfaction. Use the customer's name, remember their purchase history, and tailor your communication to their needs.

## Managing Customer Feedback

Customer feedback, whether positive or negative, is a valuable resource for your business. It helps you understand what you're doing well and where you can improve. Here's how to manage it:

1. Encourage Feedback: Actively ask your customers for their feedback through surveys, reviews, or social media.
2. Respond to Reviews: Thank customers for positive reviews and address any issues mentioned in negative reviews.
3. Act on Feedback: Use the feedback you receive to improve your products and services.

Remember, customer service doesn't end once a purchase is made. The post-purchase experience is just as important, and exceptional customer service can turn a one-time buyer into a loyal customer. In the final chapter, we'll discuss how to analyze your e-commerce store's performance and make data-driven decisions.

# Chapter 9

Analytics and Data-Driven Decisions: Gauging Your E-commerce Store's Performance

Understanding your store's performance and making data-driven decisions are integral parts of building and expanding an e-commerce business. By tracking key metrics and employing e-commerce analytics tools, you can gain insights about customers, products, marketing efforts and customer acquisition techniques that allow for informed decisions about customers, products and marketing tactics - empowering informed growth decisions. This chapter will walk you through setting up analytics solutions, understanding key metrics and using this data for growth purposes.

**Establish E-commerce Analytics**

For accurate tracking of store performance, Google Analytics is an indispensable and free solution. To begin tracking it:

1. Create a Google Analytics Account: If you do not already have one, create one in order to sign up with Google Analytics.
2. Set Up A Property For Your Ecommerce Store: A property represents your website where data for reports will be compiled by Google Analytics.

3. Enable Ecommerce Tracking: From the View column, navigate to Ecommerce Settings and enable E-commerce Tracking by toggling "Enable E-commerce."

**Understanding Key Metrics**

Once you've set up analytics, you can start tracking a variety of metrics. Here are some key metrics to monitor:

1. Traffic: This refers to the number of people visiting your website.
2. Bounce Rate: This is the percentage of visitors who leave your site after viewing only one page.
3. Conversion Rate: This is the percentage of visitors who make a purchase.
4. Average Order Value (AOV): This is the average amount spent each time a customer places an order.
5. Customer Lifetime Value (CLV): This is the total amount of money a customer is expected to spend in your store during their lifetime.
6. Cart Abandonment Rate: This is the percentage of customers who add items to their cart but don't complete the purchase.

**Utilizing Data to Drive Growth**

Once you have access to your analytics data, you can use it to drive growth. For instance, if your bounce rate is too high, improving design or user experience might help; while if conversion rate drops low enough you could experiment with CTAs or offer more appealing product descriptions may increase conversion.

Understanding your AOV and CLV can help you decide the optimal amount to spend acquiring new customers, while an increase in cart abandonment rate might necessitate an email recovery campaign or streamlining checkout processes.

Running an effective e-commerce store requires careful strategic planning, outstanding customer service, effective marketing campaigns and data-driven decision making. By following a commitment to continuous learning and improvement you can build an e-commerce business that not only achieves financial success but also makes an important impactful statement about what kind of impactful products and services your brand can make in customers' lives.

# Chapter 10

## Scaling Your E-commerce Store: Planning for Future Growth

 Growing and scaling your e-commerce business is the next step after successfully establishing it. This phase involves building on the solid foundation you've created and strategically increasing your operational capacity to accommodate increased demand without compromising the quality of your products or customer service. In this chapter, we'll explore strategies for scaling, including expanding product offerings, entering new markets, optimizing operations, and using advanced technologies.

### Expand Your Product Offerings Now

Extending your product line can draw in new customers and increase sales. When considering adding new items, make sure they fit with your brand and meet customer needs; customer feedback, market research, and sales data can all help identify potential new offerings.

### Entering New Markets

Expanding geographically can significantly grow your customer base. This could involve selling internationally or targeting new local regions. Before you expand, research these markets to understand local consumer behavior, competition, and any legal or logistical considerations.

**Optimization of Operations**

As your business expands, optimizing operations may become necessary in order to meet increased demands. This might involve outsourcing certain tasks or automating processes as needed or purchasing better software and equipment.

**Leveraging Advanced Technologies**

1. Advanced technologies can improve your customer experience and operational efficiency. For example:
2. Artificial Intelligence (AI): AI can personalize the shopping experience, automate customer service through chatbots, and provide predictive analytics to forecast sales and manage inventory.
3. Augmented Reality (AR): AR can provide interactive shopping experiences, such as virtual try-ons or product visualizations.
4. Blockchain: Blockchain can improve supply chain transparency, enhance security, and simplify transactions.

**Building Partnerships**

Forming strategic partnerships can help you access new customers, expand your product range, or improve your service. This might involve partnering with complementary businesses, influencers, or thought leaders in your industry.

## Continual Learning and Adaptation

Finally, remember that growing a business is an ongoing process that requires continuous learning, adaptation, and innovation. Stay current with industry trends, customer behavior, and technological advancements. Regularly revisit and refine your business strategy, and don't be afraid to take calculated risks to propel your business forward.

Scaling your e-commerce store is a challenging yet exciting journey. With careful planning, strategic decision-making, and a customer-centric approach, you can grow your business and achieve new levels of success. Remember, the sky's the limit, so dream big and work hard to make those dreams a reality.

# Chapter 11

Preparing for the Unexpected: Risk Management and Contingency Planning

Running an e-commerce business can present many unique challenges. Unexpected events may arise that disrupt operations, damage your reputation or negatively affect sales. Therefore, having an effective risk management plan in place is absolutely essential - this chapter will guide you through identifying potential risks, developing contingency plans and implementing successful risk mitigation strategies.

**Identifying Potential Risks**

Every business faces different risks, depending on its size, industry, location, and other factors. Common risks for e-commerce businesses include:

1. Technical Issues: Problems with your website, payment gateway, or other systems could disrupt your operations or deter customers.
2. Security Breaches: Cyber-attacks or data breaches can compromise your customers' personal information and damage your reputation.
3. Supply Chain Disruptions: Issues with suppliers or logistics providers can impact your ability to deliver products to customers.
4. Regulatory Changes: New laws or regulations could affect how you do business.

**Contingency Plans in Excel**

1. Once you've identified potential risks, devise contingency plans to address how they will be addressed should such situations arise. These should include:
2. Response Strategy: Establish how you will address and reduce any negative effects from an issue or crisis, while the Communication Plan details how your team, customers, suppliers, and other stakeholders will communicate during any crisis situation.
3. Recovery Plan: Create an action plan for returning normal operations after the crisis has subsided.

**Implementing Risk Management Strategies**

Beyond creating contingency plans, there are proactive strategies you can implement to manage risks:

1. Regular Maintenance and Updates: Regularly update and maintain your website and systems to prevent technical issues and protect against cyber threats.
2. Security Measures: Implement robust security measures, like secure sockets layer (SSL) encryption, firewalls, and two-factor authentication, to protect your customers' data.
3. Diversified Suppliers: Don't rely too heavily on a single supplier. Having multiple suppliers can protect you against supply chain disruptions.
4. Legal Compliance: Stay informed about relevant laws and regulations to ensure your business remains compliant.

Preparing for the unexpected might seem like an intimidating task, but it is an integral component of running an effective e-commerce business. By identifying potential risks and creating contingency plans as well as proactive strategies, you can safeguard against potential threats to ensure long-term success for your e-commerce enterprise - hence the saying, 'hope for the best, but plan for worst."

# Conclusion

## Embracing the Journey of E-commerce Success

E-commerce is more than a platform for buying and selling products online; it's an engaging, innovative business model that continues to change how we shop. As we have explored in this book, building a successful e-commerce store involves multiple components - initial planning and research; choosing an appropriate platform; designing a user-friendly website; effectively marketing products; providing great customer service; making data-driven decisions; scaling operations as needed; scaling operations further as needed and being prepared for unexpected circumstances.

Yet, amidst the logistics, the planning, the analysis, and the strategy, it's essential to remember the human element in e-commerce. Behind every click, every purchase, and every review is a person. Ensuring that the customer remains at the heart of your e-commerce business will set you apart in an increasingly crowded digital marketplace.

Furthermore, it's crucial to realize that e-commerce success is not an immediate journey; rather it involves planning, implementing, reviewing and refining. Mistakes and setbacks will occur, but they provide invaluable opportunities for learning which can drive growth and innovation.

As you embark on or continue your e-commerce journey, we hope this book provides a helpful roadmap. But remember, this is your journey. Use the principles and strategies outlined in this book as a starting point, but don't be afraid to innovate, experiment, and forge your own path.

May the future of your e-commerce venture be bright, successful, and rewarding. After all, your success story is just beginning.

www.ingramcontent.com/pod-product-compliance
Lightning Source LLC
Chambersburg PA
CBHW080815220526
45466CB00011BB/3575